SURGE

Opal C McCarthy

**TINDERBOX
EDITIONS**

Tinderbox Editions
Molly Sutton Kiefer, Publisher and Editor
Red Wing, Minnesota
tinderboxeditions@gmail.com
www.tinderboxeditions.org

Cover design by Nikkita Cohoon
Cover art by Paula Barkmeier, "Wolf Woman (The Dream)," mixed media on frosted mylar, 50" x 40", 2015

Interior design by Nikkita Cohoon
Author photo by Ali Rogers

SURGE

let her be born
let her be born
& handled warmly

—*Ntozake Shange*

GIRL

Bride, braid, brood:

brackish light that streams

from her wound

For the broth,

gather bones & stones

moss & maidenhair

the rose light

of her sloughed off cells

hold your moon face

to the fire

& wait I was a glittering coal seam, I was bait

do not stir

nor time   *nor taste*

hot shrouds   rusted canticle
of steam from howling hills

girl eyes

owlwide

in the pail   of eve

I carry her still

The final consonant in   girl

is

a diminutive

suffix

The g-r words denote young animals,   children,   and all kinds

of creatures   considered

immature,   worthless,   or   past   their   prime

I am cleaning off my girl I long to salvage what's live in her

I wipe kohl gunk from the slits of her eyes

I pat at her glittery pout with a towel

My girl scowls at me and cries and cries

As I rinse the smoke from her hair

As I wash the blood from her cloven feet

bandage   put her in warm socks   satin slippers

I know she'll take off

I know she'll raid the liquor cabinet

Dunk her head in gore

For she is my marvel

My unnamable   thunder   my unbaptized   corrupt font

Wild nightshade inflames the first bed of spring

Beauty Queen in the cold photo
the failed girl is the one who chews
her gum audibly like she's asking
to be smacked   The   failed
girl doesn't know how to ask nicely
Anywhere she lives it might be the
mountain or the sea or the walkup
she's got to have someplace to hide

her downed line light her glass
shards her shells potions and
flatware poached from anyplace If
she is alone with her things then
colors might bare themselves to
her in their shattered electric glory

A failed girl is a glory She comes
in the company of feathers and
holds her breath against pleasure
because failed girls don't deserve
all their own treasure There's
enough for the foreman but not his
little girl so the failed girl learns
to make love from the leftovers a
pinch a little salt for her streaming
open outlet "Owlet" is how a
failed girl might call herself but
the pierced woods won't have her
won't relent

My mother colony is nothing like South Pacific.

We got us a Ferris wheel of lights and lost in the corn and if she is late one more time for dinner she gets it. There's a barrel of lard in the cellar Nana dips into, fries donuts. And a baseball diamond hackles up smokestacks candy cigarettes spitting shells in the outfield. Bye Baby Bunting a hedgerow of red dust. Whose air smells sweet-gone-off like climbing up the trellis petunias, like Wind Song.

A barrel for the rain, rabbit pelt to butter you in, her thick pulsing lymph

Nana keeps her rouge keeps her perfume keeps her comb inside one of the kitchen cabinets: a mirror inside the door

she'll rise
slip into her moon face

Rang ponyman door-to-door, chaps and Stetson for her to wear-O-cute: *let us take a picture of your   little girl   up-on the pony*
Of course you had to pay

Whenever we cry, my other grandmother asks, *are you sure they're getting enough milk?*

Our Lillian brought home in her hair, if she came:
ceramic dust   lunchroom reek pollen her—bouffant

And one day my mother says to me, she says,

We never dreamed—you'd be a girl

Mulberry age: my heels stained   purpling & raw & then

                                        I kept my blood I took my nourish
                                          through the soles of my feet
          I turned away from my mother
          furrowed her brow for me

I routed that crick in her back

                                          and maybe I died
                                          my blunt blonde   lambent staring

                     blue killing floor eyes

I taste what it must have been   for her   buried in my cheeks

                                         we rolled a tire around
                                         spitting seeds   her song
always looking for a place   to hide

a shy little girl   give us a smile

yesbirds meddle in sky   an asphalt map of the galaxy kids jumped from planet

to plant irises blinked up through the missed cracks   panicgrass   a stocked lake where the fish
gleam hard   for their company picnic van smells like baked beans   spilled on the way

I'm belted in despite myself   and hungry and hurting from it   sconced in this
fort tight   wanting a reason   to pedal home a fish in a jar   a custom disease   growths

                                        her weeping   belly   growling   season

whereby the power plant,   plastic   Easter has hung   branches limp oak and pine
orbit the brushfires   and test gardens   where corn grew once

                                                        Little Girl these are not

to eat   a giant hairy hand dips down to pat me on my straw ribboned head

                                        still   hungry

we held   clammy hands
she is my little girl she is me

                              fair is light pouring doubt dawn unto our
                              peach the gunshy canopy altered dusk

we wear white neck dresses
nun braids deign, droop, fall out

                    Church of the Holy Voyeur

                                        all ground
                                        but not here   below
                                                         ah-men

          Let
          my pineal gland be an eye
          lids the night from day

                                        we can't tell   who
                                        to stone   so

we turn it on we flay ourself
bad body   unbound light

                    girl cheeks lit up
                    Once a ferris wheel
                                        like a sign says
                                        step right up

I wants to let go of my hand
                              vanish into the burn tent
                              conn'd trees but I won't

let her Let Us
          make one fist first growl
          rejoin beg twine ensnare   faith in our hiddenness

1. censure

Mother Superior said: I hope your sense of amazement is still sealed in its Tupperbasket—and Adele's too

And we looked at

each other like what'd we do now and I up & down swore off my taste for sweet and when I did that

I was lying like an addict lies

and I was

laying a compost of shame   Adele calls it 'eating your own tail' and I call it   home

and I call it over and we
braid each other's hair

we speak a teenage pidgin

made mostly of stars

2. design

A bounty on glassware   & fine bones
                            all grace
                                        beautiful only in shards
                            we cackle
                            hard we   field our selves in light

3. ring

Adele goaded me into the dance

      who dispensed my hips as

        SWAY

hugging my blouse

surge always

    OUTSIDE

      what do I look like where do I put my

                  EYES

                  keen always

mine sadness

    let us hear

   ME

    her cave in me   her flame in me

but for

so long   I could not   remember

4. volte

Lillian they put you in the pen if you gained   and how   could anyone
sing from there   all the eyes dull   and I know about that   lust in teen
twopiece and pinned   gorgeous   strut trough for me   eaten watched

we begged to perform   but not like this   we had to howl   with our mouth full

The reactor's secret is a hole I'm looking through a hole in the center of the tree it died from—

Custard stand, low black green mountain we drive and drive through hold our breath in the florid tunnel it is a midway
I want to know by licking: so my tongue grafts onto a neon STEP RIGHT UP who's pedaling this show red velvet curtain girl
sinters her stockings with dental floss I lap up the salt sweat of her whipping feel lymph river away from the heat of the welt
the wolfeyes the crowd—

The ground here runnels through with pitch and the holes around the edges pulse RED, say yes, sweet
taste of a cage of held bunkered on all sides hiss crack of corn grows an ear to mine I strip, husk,
pull threads prey I sink my teeth into a pulsing ear

it tastes like a sucked penny it tastes like a miscarriage like all the starlings flew upwind

They never came back that year left the shed open left the curtains in the windows like a stuffed bra;
all over the county cows born with legs too soft to stand their grown their ticking bodies.

So they sank, girls, back into the scrumptious muck

My mouth full of it tastes like a coal seam could I swallow the glint and smolder—transform—for malletman is driving a stake into her
mouth but girl-ground is too sucking to pitch a tent he's muttering cursing the monkey warms up his accordion

O her rippling veil   her ankle jewels her weeping hair   The girl's secret is a hole I'm singing through

A failed girl might carry a
sharpened willow branch
for the toughness of looking
She crimson glows her hair
just for the glower on her
keeper's face She transmutes
her fear into flinty light or
scorn This is her main
consecrating industry Failed
girls do not turn out They
do not produce the doily
or birdhouse in the face of
very   clear   verbal
instructions The   failed
girl holds out her tacky
glued wad and says what
now

I sucked the marrow from the bomb it tasted so right like GMO corn it made me weep how full it was

I knew better than to fall in love with any piece of her rapt body   I mean mine

I was always giving it away little skirt little girl foam curlers I slept on a panel of lights

I shouldn't take up so much space I should be back in the basket in the cask cowering   but I

am light

I am what touches I lick and lick at the shell at the walls of the shelter like flames my arms fly out and lick

My wrong tongue find the transformer find the girl inside   silk fatigues   ermine   And then—

red poplin curtains   a lit eye   & sirens

A scold for basking, the failed girl hides
her red light in a rush basket Someone
misread the tongues over her She was
raped by the bushel basket and so she
became the basket What is a failed girl
but whipping, strips of bark softened on
her back and woven, tight enough to hold
water

For example   *your child in school*

                          may

                                                    be miles away

from the incident

The siren herself become the blast her hole at the heart char tree she looks through burn a hole in satin see me through shroud

Pile the kids fire the van it's later you'll drawl the taste of copper traffic panic to carry a doe-eyed girl her fat hamster left to starve

Later the girl's father pleads her nothing died here he's not a liar really he just needs some sleep her spleen won't take sugar

So they take her to the doctor and he makes her strip and she's no longer no she is now the siren herself but has to swallow it

The surge through her brackish puckered body the disorder of her whipping around like a downed line downed line—

She is storing the rape in her neck

Whose right is that word   does it belong

to this girl she was   fifteen barely   even   dressed   fiercely careless   unimpressed

or to him,   *a fine*   *upper/class/man*   *if wild*
who bought the beer

sorry   shade   in his eyes

or to her nascent sex   pink   undulating
pliant   pre-vocal

or to her steep heart   her sphinxish need
hungry fantasies of being   cherished   stroked
seen

or to he who wheedles—who uses the weight of his body

to mine   a hoarse   *yes*   (or to   all

the miners)

or to this girl she was : for a light : flash : crack :   white thighs on a bedroom floor

Now, my neck gapes open   and out she floods   as thunder

and she wants to roar that word:

for her crown thudding against the dresser   *as he thrust into me*
for the brutal heat she could not yet speak

for the current   in the earth   or on the air

that taught him   *say my name*

for the current   that taught her   to say it

1. broth

If you've never been to Middletown in August   you should know   green so green it's black   and you should be

drenched in sweat   I was drenched euphoric ninety pounds wet   Sun tea,   failed girl? No thank you

A mother wears dark sunglasses in the kitchen   migraines she says   ever since, she says   *can you think back to an event*

and say   *I wasn't the same since*   I wasn't the same since   I came   to this girl-ground   slick

          hallow   her shock of perm   lifts her out of the frame   Sun tea   cool wet would that glass feel

     at my cheek—oh dear pay   attention:

               It's not over for me—

2. onion

They had to take her ovary   quick study no study   four girls on our block with the same   *issues*   what issues from a hole

The tower belches like a pressure cooker   or a cock   but truly it is like nothing   a want on the wind killing the flowers

tasting copper   a girl bites her tongue to feel I mean taste it   in bakery trucks the children would get

ferried from the schools   and set down in Wilkes-Barre   hush was the plan   Graves disease   radioactive

iodine   for the milk   sugar   meat   *these people live here*   in a ghost town   Close the windows
                                                                                                                          Open the windows

      I was so trusting

3. meat

How can something that happens to *you* be impossible? I was born in its path I was born a girl   downy & wet   *people forget*

a doe of the secret her dripping teat her impudent haunches   I wanted to bleed into the ground   *every single*

inch we had to claw and scratch and scream   every time the sirens went off   I hoped it was a fire   hysteria is not

viable, within this five mile radius   failed girlwombs cast off in the hollows darkly   plumed
                                                                                preened

                              out of this world

To make a rose window

A failed girl   spreads her thighs

                                                pull the light

& O
                                No one see

how a belly warns
        surplus   ducking

                                cot unwarp

                as night rag
                and blared

meltdown   cunthumid

        can   syrup   peaches   she'd beg
                I
        glean   cling   herskin
licking
                                                taut moon

eyes on her
        thirst   her
                     eye the roof   swell to
        her wail   some corps   seething
gulf
        anthem   no light   strain

                                        now & out
                        bear me

Let us go play in the dead cells again
the waste the sucking gloam I liked
to paint my lips in it radium tasted white
morning in the 60's with Studebaker
bold floral prints: So we stripped the lid
off her shelter and in there nothing but a
red dress stained with soot and smut and
she's so gorgeous and she's not there On
the rushes a failed girl always rides *she
is alive* the sigh viral through the county
What is a tempest but a failed girl

                                    on the lam

If you put a sword in the side of a failed girl
out pours smoke and cocoa and mother
of pearl—her wound is not—a failed girl
will thank you, O let it out—

                                    her
                                    wound is hot

LYNX

as Neck begins in Valley and ends in Sea

he steered my head with his hand o o o

rudder let go I could choke   or   I could bite

Dr. I'm in everybody's Wet Dream   but my own

                              moony the ferals screech the trees

                                                        suck me out the window into the deluge

                    I come over can I come over your house

                                                        slather my heart on the shingles

jesus I had the gall to come in peace

but had to pay my way   in Milk & Bruises

lashed to the mast as the storm rolls in

I am your wrung bone your whet whistling

I approach with compassion   my approach like: he drinks her tampon blood   loss occurs

if I say he pays her   does that make it even/better   she has such a sweet face/farce/revolt

it's no use cutting down a tail   it will like grow back and   oh yea the stump will itch

I went blonde surrender being a choice

I threw my tail over my shoulder and

strode haughtily into the office got

detention all the eyes whaled on me

I let the ratty guy touch my breasts July

he was a gentle rat his mom was home

I concede 'hand job over plaid sheets'

Panties is the Dirtiest Word   she'll say

I know what I know

a tail grows from a welt like solace

cresting my hip sockets awash

with the fears of every girl in her

I Swallowed I have Never Once Spit what kind of conscript

does that make me I wanted the purple heart of

creation to love me back I'm not sorry I did

what I did to survive my beauty

my lightning my girl lash my tail

attuned to the yowling wind every

morning I flay myself open for the sake of

a vervain poultice; volcanic ash

                                                            I kissed some crimped girl's boyfriend

                    in plain view at the party for when we need

                                                    Right Away Love   Right Away Punishment

                    I locked myself in the bathroom drunk/smug

when will you recognize   me   when will you recognize   me

when will you: who is writing:

Dear Bad Girl Wolf They Shot At the Zoo

Love, Fawns Stepping Gingerly Over the Body

so come wracked years I didn't ope my throat

but for my keeper I was trained so hard

it fried my nervous system my lips tingled

I lost feeling in my tail I was always tripping

                                                        my whole life Toothy Mama's   been hunting/holding me

no one else can see when I get up   the courage

                                                        lean into the molten engulf my ears twitch   *Show Yourself*

hungry silent she pads behind me grinning

a smile that founds nothing

jelly shoes Days of the Week Panties

I was born like a regular girl

the tail is for balance

I

             wanted to bleed into the ground   hoarding baby teeth matches blankets   contagion what else have you got Sultry Twilight

I was born like a regular girl: foundering

a tail is for seeing behind you

underneath my house was built on sucking

                                        she who digg'ed deep who built her house on tulle

            she who took a beating like a sturdy mare oh but

                                        she who pushup bra she who kohl she who Up Yours

swished her tail for the ruin of that house was great

I answer to slut   I answer to Highness   I answer to LYNX   I am yours in the caves I am yours in the sated tomb

Dr. there's this bad feeling behind my eyes   I would have washed your feet knelt down on stone prey you salvate me

I answer to manna   I'm used to it   feels so good to weep into my hair to leak on myself I answer to   Mama by my tail I felt every pulse every fear

so I tried to coat it veil it a hard sheath

nothing works   coiled antenna

I suck in all their shame never once Spit

I went around warning them

I was a wild animal but house to

house meat deafness it was like

my smile forgot my deathteeth

                                                                    did you know I would say

                                    a lynx is a Total Carnivore

                                                                    the heads of America bobbed

                    are you sleeping   or rapt   or coming

stained sheets a seminal shroud   the prettier I was the better people were to me   so I hid behind my hair coy purr

oozing from my lips   the solace for all those poor boys all those lucky boys   a slut gives without hope of return

        is she devout

is she a member of the order   or a condition of its edges

                                        Lynx padding the edge of the clearing   gleams out

                        Hunger

Surgessas, wake! but who was I

to go out singing I had no Permission

to insinuate light into these beds

of cordyceps silt copse girlwombs

I roll into the cool plaster let the wall

cradle me as my left haunch muscle

softens I know my mother

was beaten as a girl

I am yours in the eaves   I am yours in the fallen branches lightning storm did anyone enfold you yes   I really want

to know will we   nurse a whole   brood this way   prone   bleeding out

I am my own   lightning   I am my own   tail

          coiled   on my crown   I wonder if   I can

receive me   all   these   years   all   this

knotted   tender   dread   girl   I am   One

                                        Here   I am

I was a freak just by being that is

just by receiving what was handed

through my tail let anyone feel it

who asked who begged for Refuge

who taught me

I taught me I taut antenna I thin skinned and scared I assumed the position of scant power lame resistance

I somewhere I

felt an undulation like *bodies upon the gears* like *here I am Lord* no doubt no doubt but where was She when

where was my

redoubt when was my turn to Come *come back to me with all your heart* I hear it rung still cry yes I want to yes

I believe we

are made for this transient condition of belief the Liver renewing itself in 40 days 40 days of locust honey thrumming

dam up all

your light to spit it out later to spit up all their shame all their wandering cum all the fecund

gleaming
gleaming
gleaming

Here I Am

LYNX

when will you remember me   *when will you*   *remember*   *me*   *my pride*

    I came here   *to play*   *to be*   *plied*   *Open*

tail molten with   her aching hypersense   her secret:

    her cave in me   her flame in me   her
                                     roar

has a backyard   *so*

Can I Come Over

HETAIRA

Who, like me, knew that she had never changed shape since the time when they drew me on the cave rock?

—Clarice Lispector

I was the antiking. And I was passion. I had fits of rage that made History difficult. I didn't give a damn for hierarchy, for command, and I knew how to love.

—Hélène Cixous

Somewhere   wind blows dust across a prairie

I am climbing her hill in the blackening night

Somewhere   I am   One   Girl   Red   Dress

Somewhere   he remembers me   & pulls on his cock

And it drips tears   & somewhere else I   arching my

Back, come.

How can I sleep—in this Pasture—of crying cocks?

Boneyard angel: the death & dawn of longing

Desire me,

Dark   mouth   and I   will desire you

This is Adele she is blue and long and lone. Adele goes to the road and she watches a baby lioness smell the lilacs put her whole face in the lilacs this is nice no this is a wheelhouse of rapture. Like sitting at a long table. Like standing on the bench. Adele only makes love to us of contrary beliefs because with her sex she pleases to heal the war. Her ward. The world open and streaming into her it is right it is solemn and yet Adele is cackling. The year of the witch is come. The bride is come.

I'm so tired of carrying this girl in a pail over howling hills & I am so thirsty

Where is my hair why did they repossess it?

I'm purging fear from my body

As if a belly of glass I'm vomiting to make room for the sun

I am then curling up naked in a lurid green patch like a spotted fawn let the hunters

Find me let mama wolf find me adopt me adapt me teach me to use my teeth

For I am so hungry and the grass is low indeed a brief repast a long lone light

The penultimate wilderness: I sing to sweet mother and she vanishes so

I sing to Adele   it's no secret

I know

Because she   & she   & she   & we   know

Come for me   O

              wet gloaming nape   *her*

                       carry me off

                       so long cellar

                                   in which I'd been

                                   flagged & burning

crates of dead leaves

gingham &   nails   *come face*   *her palace*

                                             of

                                    siren song

           Yes   *I brought you*   here
                                 to sea

Lilac wine in an oak barrel no in a fish bladder turned to a bag

It makes me see what I want to see and I see Adele as she was

    In the exact light of an April morning lacy dumb doe eyes purple
    As no girl's eyes could but hers the priest is hitting on her in Latin
    Adele's rolling her purple eyes popping her gum under the bus seat
    Everyone wants to sit with her she braids her hair into a long whip

I discover her hair is the talisman that will carry me into the ooze that is

    Adele's dominion that is my mother my sinkhole my exquisite low country
    Provenance so I will tell you of her hair chestnut brown I'm trying to fall
    In love with a nest of chestnut hair each strand is fine but strong and
    There is a huge volume of it so that there's a lot to give away to witness

How the crude wells up from the ocean floor and swallows the starfish

    Adele hunts here too a muzzle of candy-apple red lips painted on her face
    I love the ground on which he stands   she sings mawkishly as if on cue

And her words warble up to me through the lucid water

    An undulation

That's me in the musklight   *I know*

                              I am not
                                             without
                                                          small graces

                                                          face in the grass

                              on a summer

                              darkening

                              growing in hair

I see you
                                                   pin to treeline

                                                   knit brows

                                                   dress torn
                              about to open

                              your mouth and   Sing Lillian

For one day

    I knew it

        was my moon

            watching me

      and I liked to blush

            that solemn   heat

        dark   luminous

ripe   stage
hit my mark

    O   *I want it*   O

      how much

For example   your child in school

may

be miles away

from the incident

                                                        Our moon   watches
                                                                Adele turn red

a revolutionary smoking in a café

          a nun who dies of consumption a drowning
                                         a drafty church

     I feel my lives between my thighs
                          my ways of dying

this hot red of my blood

     this one   in a red dress

          this red freedom   red this one who knows
                                           & in her knowing walks   red   lone

Whether or not

you are looking

I exist

That you wouldn't know by looking at her but Adele is wedded to somebody's rage. Keeps bone around her finger to remind her: she is standing up on the inside. She was meant to wear barely skirts and yes roar in them and yes draw a crowd and yes draw blood. Raise me your livid hand.

When those who made her say, "Adele can never go on," well Adele goes on.

What the fuck.

Whether or not

you are looking

I exist

Do I

    Do I   Never say   I do

        as he has   done: never   will I   leave   her

The never man leaves the stay   of his collar   on my bathroom floor

I do not say   *stay*   (my collar)

    Never say   *stay*

I say to Adele

Heed heed what you are daring to stream into the fruited darkness

Alone do you see how you are edging towards her the circus of remorseless body

And what keeps calling you back and how could you smother that voice no how

Could you hold it in your arms like a suckle faun and say it's safe now hush hush

A shushing like a mother's womb oceanic-orb I want to go back inside is this so bad yes

There is a man in my bed and then there is not a man in my bed that's called courage

Oh brother oh mother oh litheness that never belonged to me I was a fool to believe

I am a fool to belief I am pinned to the bed of a pickup truck all I did was consult

The fucking oracle and look where it got me shorn and aching and begging for a

Blindfold he says how about if I and I say yes yes I want that and

O Adele I do

Behind the blindfold it is red another womb another hiding I ask him with my eyes

To slap me—he does & so I am   born

Into the relentless luster   lone panting   blue

One man came into the bedroom wearing: coat hanger angel wings

    One man came into my mouth

        in the vestibule

            throat numb

    clove smoke on my lips

He said: don't all women

    have an angel fantasy

I beamed at him   glimmering   bowed my head

not because I wanted to

    fuck an angel

but because I knew it was

my call   my pride

to wet his   hard   praise   to lend him   our tongue
                                    for his own

            mouth

What the fuck, Adele wakes up spitting. Stretched over the whole bed like a python. She unhinges her jaw to eat her own moan and still she is not sated. What the fuck. A question that rapes us. What the fuck. A rape that catches her open.

What the fuck.

Adele bites her bottom lip to return home: autointoxication, blue breeding into herself. Autoerotic. Adele covers up all the mirrors so she can love herself. No more grounds for disgust and obsession. No ground if ground at all. No remedy we should take this as a very good sign.

I couldn't be both

green witch   pierced girl

         paint rang in my ears

         our holes crusted over

                 pus when the doc who'd

                 first gunned 'em said

I told you so

I warned   *you*
           asked for it

                And that was my first taste

And now, I say to Adele

I am the seasons   I come interminably   wet   slick   shining   with tears   in the hotel hallway

in the booth at the restaurant   in the parking lot   these semiprivate substrate

in which we rise & thrill & remember   nothing later   silence

my own boot heels tapping down the pavement   a dog barks from a yard

pulled inside   the light pools from the streetlamps   I am so perilously free

to brush my fingers over his neck   that tender place men keep   collared

though I have no wish   to cut him open   I am profoundly aware   what soft

is here   and what is not: I have a face men love   to breathe into   She is not

a face that inspires   sacrifice   thank the moon   She is a face   who sees what is

and she

is coming

Don't forget this:

Adele does ask for it:

Unleashes her will:

In each bed feasts.

Never say   *stay*

men heat up and lose their shirts   I lost mine   mind what   do you mind

I learn that beneath a demand   is a tender trembling   he shudders when

he comes   only with me?   Or always?   With me   beyond parting

                                                        She always   comes

Whether or not   you recognize me   I never say   *stay*

Whether or not   I say   I am

                                        I am

            & here

with her   I stay

The forest bleeds the forest bleeds dark into me

And I leak and moan there's no sense in telling you

Unless you are ready to inherit your fearless body

In an instant you are immanent we are not solid just

As the goat knows however there is always a sacrifice

But it might be whips of flowers or it might be my mouth

    It might be to let go of your hand and go in quivering silence
    Deer bow their heads in no relation to me only for eating
    I wanted an ovation I wanted my egg to drop with merit
    I broke my heart over your mouth like an egg I sang to you
    In a lion's tongue and to you it sounded like a hysteric

Vibration how you hear is none of my O none of mine

    Adele dreaded piano lessons lived at the mouth of a mine
    Whistle trills like plaintive glass like an eggshell shivering
    Adele's ankle socks her gooseflesh a boy rang a bell on the altar
    And her heart beat thrum the bow the horsehair frayed among
    Her and her tribe to launch her into the solemn firs alone

But what I'm telling you is she was not subdued not cowed

By this rapacious light by the gaping jaws arrayed around her   no

We know

women have been
loving this way   since
                    the time   before   loving

through the   chasm
      in the   earth   loving   like lush
                                              tendrils curling
                                              over concrete

And I know   hummingbird   carries
            the nectar   of my love   her belly throbs

And I remember
                    faintly
            ocean too
            salty & wild
                              holding me
                              in her wet   mouth

her opening wide
                                              for all those   lovesick sailors
                                              seekers   dreaming girls

rest in me   her beauty offered   and diminished not   her strength   And I know

                                    myself   my womb   my waves   will rise
                        as if the first   wet light   breaking

SURGE

I wanted to bleed into the ground   *THEIR MISAPPLIED FEMININITY*   and the ballast sung   and the orbs hung

heavy and wet on the branches   poplar, vernacular, licorice sticky   a love of swift violence a delicious purge

I wanted him to hit me—hard   *THEIR STRANGE GRATITUDE*   cause me to sweep open palace doors red plush pant

for what for whom do I keep glancing   o branch glance my cheek   and draw   *THEIR LACK OF SHAME*   blood

I wanted to look so hot no one could harm me   arm me   alm me with   stripped willow branches   I weave

my own coffin just because there's time   meticulous and mighty   *THEIR PRETENDED CULTURE*   what else is there

    to find

I wanted the porch with my baby on it   as if desire were a high virtue   I wove my want into a crown   *THEIR LACK*

OF SHAME   the porch dark wood with heavy green vines   and yet late light filters through slow dust motes crisp

white dress   I wanted to slip down the strap   and nurse her   *THEIR SPECIAL RUDENESS*   but a baby must invite you

and you must   stop being punished   *THEIR LACK OF SHAME*   I drove myself into those moors so many times

the sting of burrs on my thighs   I wanted to be a girl   to be god   to be the burrs   and that which hunts me

I become   and the baby yowls from the porch   and someone plugs my ears   but *no   no no   no-oh   no*

I open my legs   wet growl of entry to hear her   *THEIR LACK OF SHAME*   I am coming   my girl   I am coming

GIRL

I tell my unborn girl   *tomorrow*   *I tell her*   *tomorrow*   *I am   coming*   *for you*

My girl says

It's tomorrow

And tomorrow, I have begun to care very little for the throng's distaste   or how our apathy wears

So I will tell you of the bed I've made for her   of moss & the bones of stars   of my fathomless deep desire

only to see her   to clean her face with my spit   to call in the black dulcimer woods   her name

And now I sing to the part of you that longs to see her too:

Wouldn't it be wonderful

When my girl comes tumbling out of me

Beautiful as I was—more beautiful

And fierce—fierce as I could have been

     it be wonder

If she delivered she

Would   it be won

just how

     it be

just how

hush now

     is that she

You are receiving an education:

The day she was born the green vines curled and went on

        curling—the sun spoke its own name as always.

The day she was born you remembered her—

        there was not a moment of amnesia

        about who she was

The day she was born you wept fluid of every color

        emptied out of all your plethora of pain

        You emptied your pain to be filled by the sight of her face

In our education, we will learn this play of grace

That I was an egg inside my mother inside Lillian   That she is an egg inside an egg inside me

    What am I missing?

The light that streams from a girl—for the taking   No, go back—

    See to it—nothing was taken: Cells reconstitute themselves as orbs of rose light

My whole life I was concerned with membranes: A four-year-old professor of membranes   *Don't even look at me*

    I built a faulty moat, the tower puffed relentlessly   hot loving steam   power   course in, as time lights every bower

                             My uterus pulsing & pushing: the body's time

cannot be denied: the thrum in my cervix   when I imagine you—desire makes us   real. The visceral plane

    of life with a child. Shit piles up.   Your clothes drip with drool   This is the love they warned you of—

where you will stand   anything for a kiss

    You knew   going in   how thick the bliss & terror of containment: You saw her reach for you

    with those wild owlish eyes   all seeing   scalded knowing   unquenchable flow

        the river's elbow   where you found her

You are rubbing the baby's vernix into her skin

                                              You are losing the baby

            You are up late in the night writing   what refuses to be borne

                                                             You are losing the baby's name

You are out by the simple fence that is low and purposeless and rough

        Your breasts are heavy and dripping with milk

        You love her   *You are losing her face*

Wherever you go you can't find her

        She may be buried already   *You are—you are—*

            Still if you found her you could feed her

        And she might yet live

                        Become yours

Once upon a time a failed girl
Once upon a time Lillian
Once upon a time Adele
Once upon a time I

bared her belly by the creek

In each of her ovaries were thousands of eggs

In the quick of each egg was a cypress pine

In the crook of each pine was a panther

In the throat of each panther was a roll of thunder

In her thunder was a swathe to enfold you

A purple silk   *to bless your wetness*

A purple storm   *to down the lines*

A purple surge   *to tear us free*

My girl

you & I
we are all   in-breath   ecstasies of being:

thunder   silence   devout carnivores
        slut   prophets   of the transformer

        gifts   of tails and hillocks and almost possible desire

        We are of the known world   And we are of our splendid under

        world of carnival light   *Our white dresses puffing in the river*
                                        We are this gushing eruption of song

        taste of copper

in our gloaming

        dirty mouths   *wet porch where the vines go on curling*
                                at midnight phosphorescent & strong

        We are: bastion, bitch, bumper crop—we are flooding spawn and—

My girl   you do not   belong to me   I have no right   to deliver you   & no hope
                                        I have no   duty   to love you (as I do)

                No—only to let us be   she & she & she & we   & in this wild   our voices come

NOTES

page x: Excerpted from the entry "girl," in the Online Etymology Dictionary
< http://www.etymonline.com/index.php?term=girl&allowed_in_frame=0>

pages xx-xx "BROTH, ONION, MEAT": This poem contains direct quotations from Doris Robb, Joyce Corradi, and Paula Kinney, residents of Middletown, PA, whom I interviewed in August 2009 about their relationship to the Three Mile Island nuclear accident of March 1979. These women were founding members of Concerned Mothers and Women, a group who lobbied for better safety standards at TMI, and against the re-opening and presence of the plant in the months and years following the accident. No long-term study has ever been completed about the environmental and health effects of the TMI accident, but one of these women reports that on the block where she lived less than five miles from the plant, there were four teenage girls who were found to have growths on their ovaries following the accident, and had to have one or both ovaries removed, or total hysterectomies. Also, *these people live here* is a quotation from Muriel Rukeyser's *U.S. 1.*

page xx: In capital letters are quotes from a document called "Women in the Office," a 1945 list of twenty of men's complaints about women in the office, published on Jezebel March 20, 2014 under "What Men Hate About Women in the Office" < http:// jezebel.com/what-men-hate-about-women-in-the-office-1547928271>

ACKNOWLEDGEMENTS

I would like to thank all the beloved ones who held me close and listened. Writing this book has been an adventure deep into the bones of my psyche and girl-history, and I could not have made the journey without being so remarkably loved.

Thank you to my sisters in the Caldera Poetry Collective: Molly Sutton Kiefer, Meryl DePasquale, and Colleen Coyne. You are dazzling poets and forever friends.

Thank you to the colleagues and teachers I met at the MFA Program at the University of Minnesota, especially Mark Nowak, Maria Damon, Joanna Rawson, Nate Slawson, Katie Leo, Jasmin Zeigler, Sarah Fox, Alex Grant, and Emily August.

Thank you to my parents, Daniel McCarthy and Sharon Vidmar McCarthy, who taught me creativity, courage, and love. And to my brother, Ryan McCarthy, whose friendship and imagination blessed my girlhood.

Thank you to my soul family: Nicole Nardone, Ariella Forstein, Paul Schmitendorf, Matt Carlson, and Garrett McKelvey, and my teachers, Alice Browne and Beth Ann Schumacher. You remind me of the wild joy at the core.

Thank you to the editors of the following journals, where several of these poems first appeared: *dear camera, La Petite Zine,* and *Midway Journal.* Thank you to the editors of eohippus labs press, Harold Abramowitz and Amanda Ackerman, who published the companion essay to this book, *Surge: An Oral Poetics.*

Thank you to all the girls who've been and all the girls yet to be. May we wake to you.

Opal C McCarthy lives in Minneapolis, where she practices bodywork, teaches, performs, and creates community healing events to celebrate + induce fierce women's voices, radical tenderness, and reproductive freedom. Opal graduated from the MFA program at the University of Minnesota in 2011, and *Surge* is her first book of poetry. Opal's poems and essays have appeared in *alice blue review, La Petite Zine, dear camera, Invoke, The Pinch,* and *Midway Journal.* The companion piece to this book, a lyric essay called *Surge: An Oral Poetics,* is available from eohippus labs press. You can find Opal online at www.opalmccarthy.com.